Saving the
PANDAS

Rob Waring, *Series Editor*

HEINLE
CENGAGE Learning™

Australia • Brazil • Japan • Korea • Mexico • Singapore • Spain • United Kingdom • United States

Words to Know

This story starts in Chengdu [tʃʌndu], China, which is the capital city of Sichuan [sɪtʃwɑn] province. It then moves to an area near Beijing [beɪdʒɪŋ], the capital city of China.

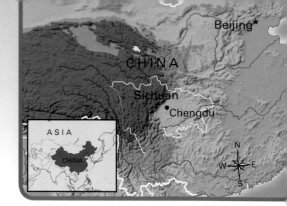

A **Panda Research.** Read the paragraph. Then complete the sentences with the correct form of the underlined words and phrases.

This story is about the conservation of giant pandas and how science may help save them. Zhihe Zhang [dʒihʌ dʒɑŋ] is a geneticist who studies pandas and their families, but it isn't an easy job. First of all, female pandas can only get pregnant during a three-day period each year. Then, after they give birth, some new mothers aren't able to take care of their young cubs properly. Because of these difficulties and others, Zhang has started a center to breed pandas and help the parents raise their babies.

1. The state of having a baby developing in one's body is to be _____.

2. _____ is the protection of animals or other natural things.

3. When a mother _____, she has a baby.

4. A _____ is a term for the baby of certain types of animals.

5. People _____ animals to make more of that same animal.

6. A _____ is a scientist who studies the passing of physical characteristics from parents to children.

Panda Facts

Height at Shoulder: 60 to 80 centimeters
Weight: 100 to 150 kilograms
Size at Birth: approximately 113 grams
Life Span: 14 to 20 years in wild; up to 30 years in zoos
Primary Food Source: bamboo
Conservation Status: endangered

B **Panda Problems.** Read the sentences. Then complete the paragraph with the correct form of the underlined words.

Bamboo is a tall plant from the grass family.
The cutting down of trees in a large area is called deforestation.
Endangered animals are so few in number that they may soon
 no longer exist.
A habitat is the natural area in which an animal or plant normally lives.
The wilderness is land in its natural state.

There are a lot of problems with maintaining the panda population. Giant pandas eat (1)_____ and so they need the forests where it grows. Due to (2)_____, many of these forests have disappeared. Many pandas have also lost their natural (3)_____ and have no place to live. Because of this, pandas are now (4)_____ and there may soon be no more left. Luckily, people in China are working hard to replant the forests and save China's (5)_____ areas for the pandas!

A Giant Panda with Its Cub

bamboo

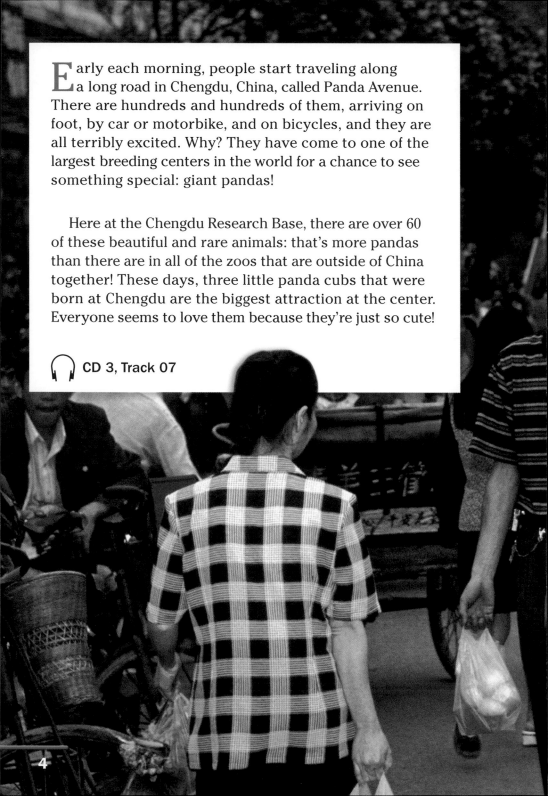

Early each morning, people start traveling along a long road in Chengdu, China, called Panda Avenue. There are hundreds and hundreds of them, arriving on foot, by car or motorbike, and on bicycles, and they are all terribly excited. Why? They have come to one of the largest breeding centers in the world for a chance to see something special: giant pandas!

Here at the Chengdu Research Base, there are over 60 of these beautiful and rare animals: that's more pandas than there are in all of the zoos that are outside of China together! These days, three little panda cubs that were born at Chengdu are the biggest attraction at the center. Everyone seems to love them because they're just so cute!

🎧 CD 3, Track 07

The task of looking after the cute little cubs belongs to a woman named **Hong Zuo**.[1] She's been taking care of panda cubs for more than 20 years and has a very special relationship with these animals. Every day, she washes the little cubs and takes care of them. And of course, with three little pandas that are full of fun, there's always room for play time. For Zuo, it's almost like being a mother. She explains, "You hold them like you [would] hold your own baby, and they play with you. I have a very special feeling about them."

---

[1]**Hong Zuo:** [hɔŋ zwoʊ]

The three little cubs spend most of their time playing and they are obviously strong and healthy. It's difficult to see it now, but the pandas are actually just getting better after a very serious illness. Originally there were four cubs at the center, but one of the cubs died from the illness. Zuo still gets emotional when she thinks about it. With tears in her eyes she says, "I still remember when this little cub died." Sometimes it's difficult to be a panda keeper, and it's always hard to lose an animal.

It's now especially important to Zuo and everyone at the center that the remaining three cubs survive. The cubs have no idea, but there are a lot of hopes and dreams that depend upon them.

Zhihe Zhang is a geneticist and director of the Chengdu Research Base. His dream is to breed pandas and to eventually release them back into the wild. The giant panda is endangered, and Zhang would like to stop them from disappearing completely from Earth. The giant panda's natural habitat is in China. Therefore, many people feel that pandas somehow represent the country. Zhang expresses this in his own words, "We Chinese call the panda our national **treasure**."[2]

Zhang then talks about why it's so important to save the giant pandas. "We think [that] as Chinese [people], it's our responsibility and **obligation**[3] to save these animals," he says. However, he then expresses his concern about the environment and how it may affect the pandas. According to Zhang, it's now especially important to help these endangered creatures because the environmental situation has gotten worse and worse.

---

[2]**treasure:** something that is very valuable; something very special
[3]**obligation:** duty or responsibility

Infer Meaning

1. How does Zhihe Zhang feel about saving the pandas?

2. What do you think he means when he says the panda is 'our national treasure'?

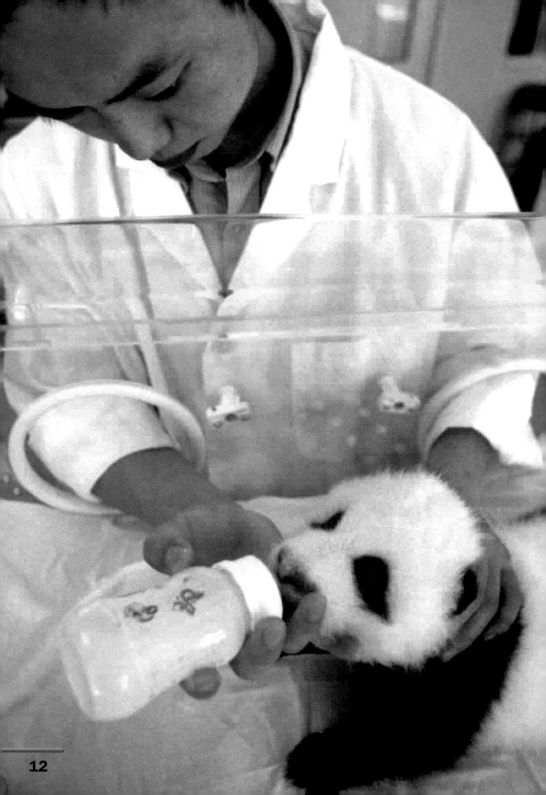

Pandas have lived on Earth for eight million years. However, Zhang believes that the present time is the most significant period in history for pandas. He also believes that it's a time when the future of giant pandas could easily change—for the better or for the worse. Something needs to be done in order to ensure the pandas' survival. Luckily, Zhang is very confident that science will be able to help.

For the most part, the **reproductive**[4] life of the giant panda is a mystery, but Zhang and his team are discovering more and more about it every day. They have also been very successful with breeding pandas at the Chengdu Research Base. The team started more than 20 years ago with only five pandas that were born in zoos. Now, years later, they've successfully bred more than 44 cubs!

---

[4]**reproductive:** of or related to producing babies or more of the same

The biggest problem in breeding pandas is that there is very little time when female pandas are able to **conceive**.[5] There is only a single period of time each year when females can get pregnant—and it lasts for only three days! In addition to this, female pandas don't easily become pregnant, even if they have an appropriate partner. Because of these issues, scientists at the center must often assist in making pregnancy possible. However, their important role in saving the pandas doesn't end there.

---

[5] **conceive:** become pregnant

Even with all of the help with the pregnancy process, it still doesn't necessarily mean that a newly born giant panda will live. Another problem with breeding and raising pandas is that they very often give birth to **twins**.[6] If that happens, the mother usually takes care of only one of her cubs and leaves the other one completely. The second cub in the pair often dies.

Now, **vets**[7] at the Chengdu Research Base have found a way to save both cubs when a mother has twins. They use a 'switch method'. They take one cub at a time and **rear**[8] it by hand. Later, they then give that cub back to its mother, and take the other cub into their care. By switching the cubs from time to time, both cubs get all of the care that they need from their mother. The process is not easy, but it's essential to save an animal that truly represents China. Panda keeper Hong Zuo thinks about that every day. As she gently holds and hugs the little pandas, she jokes, "I take care of these three cubs more carefully than I do my own babies."

---

[6]**twin:** one of two children born of the same mother at the same time
[7]**vet:** veterinarian; a doctor who takes care of animals
[8]**rear:** bring up; take care of

Fact Check

1. How many cubs do pandas often have at one time?

2. Why do panda cubs often die if the mother has more than one?

3. What can vets do to stop that from happening?

In addition to the reproductive troubles faced by giant pandas, another significant problem exists for the animal: their habitat is disappearing. Forests are being cut down all over the world, including in China. People often want to develop the land into towns and cities. As more and more deforestation occurs, less and less wilderness is available for endangered animals. This includes China's giant panda, the most famous endangered animal of them all. Pandas eat bamboo, which means that they must have plenty of forests where the plant grows. It is absolutely essential for their survival. Fortunately, people are beginning to understand this, and they're starting to make important changes.

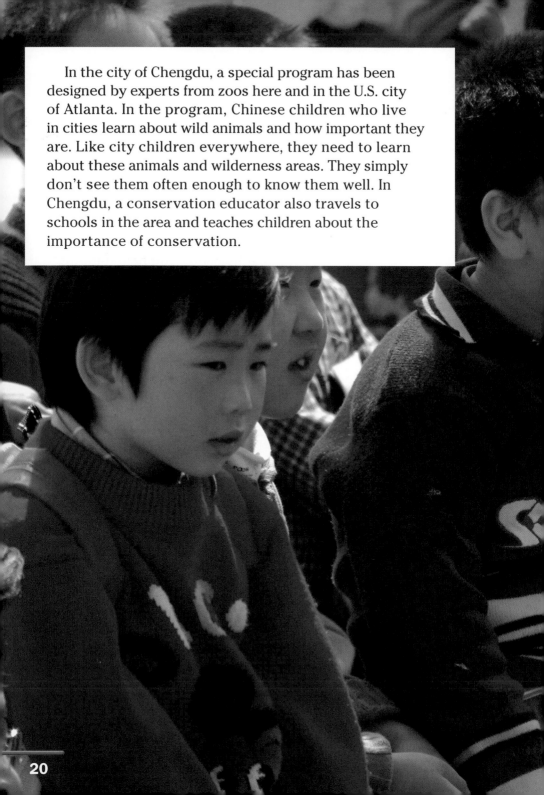

In the city of Chengdu, a special program has been designed by experts from zoos here and in the U.S. city of Atlanta. In the program, Chinese children who live in cities learn about wild animals and how important they are. Like city children everywhere, they need to learn about these animals and wilderness areas. They simply don't see them often enough to know them well. In Chengdu, a conservation educator also travels to schools in the area and teaches children about the importance of conservation.

The Chengdu conservation education program seems to be working very well. The conservation educator works with the children to sing songs about pandas and make art projects that involve them. The children also learn about other endangered animals. They enjoy being taught about the animals, and they also learn that people must work to ensure the animals' survival. One five-year-old boy in the class even says, "The human being(s) cannot hurt the pandas. They should conserve them **just like the elephants**."[9]

The education of children is one way to help save the pandas and their habitats, but what else can be done? There is another major change that has been made as well. People in China are starting to plant forests again. It is hoped that this will not only help to increase the pandas' food supply and habitat area, but also help to improve the forest conditions of the whole country.

_____

[9]**just like the elephants:** *NOTE:* Here the boy is likely referring to the fact that the Asian elephant is also an endangered species due to loss of habitat.

Forest planting programs have now been established all around China. Just two hours outside Beijing, near the Great Wall of China, big changes are occurring. A forestry expert named **Xiaoping Wang**[10] and his team are helping to **reforest**[11] the entire area. The men and women on the team are digging the earth and planting new trees all over the hillsides. Wang feels that it's very important for people to take care of the environment in this way.

---

[10] **Xiaoping Wang:** [ʃyaʊpɪŋ wɑŋ]
[11] **reforest:** plant trees in an effort to create a forest where one was lost

Wang and his team have been very successful in planting new forests near the Great Wall. The changes are quite obvious when one looks at the area. In the recent past, forests covered only two percent of the region. Now, the amount of tree cover has increased to 44 percent. New trees are growing everywhere, and the countryside is colorful once again.

Wang's project is just one of six major projects that are designed to reforest the countryside of China. They are also designed to rebuild natural environments for animals like the giant panda. The panda is an animal that has represented China for centuries. Now, many people in China are working hard to save this beautiful animal for everyone's future.

What do you think?

1. Do you think the giant panda will survive? Why or why not?

2. Which project will help the pandas the most: the breeding program, the education program, or the reforestation program? Why do you feel that way?

After You Read

1. Why does the writer give details about people walking and bicycling on Panda Avenue?
   A. to show methods of exercising in China
   B. to show how popular pandas are
   C. to describe an unknown area of China
   D. to explain that the research base is far from the city

2. According to page 6, which of the following is NOT one of Hong Zuo's responsibilities?
   A. breeding pandas
   B. washing pandas
   C. playing with pandas
   D. holding pandas

3. What do the three cubs represent to the people at Chengdu Research Base?
   A. an opportunity for China's geneticists to become famous
   B. a chance to show the world their center
   C. an opportunity to research why pandas die
   D. a chance for the panda species to stop being endangered

4. What view does Zhihe Zhang express on page 10?
   A. Since pandas live in China, his country must help protect them.
   B. The world believes only China can save the pandas.
   C. The environmental situation for pandas is improving.
   D. The obligation to help pandas is too big for Chinese people.

5. The word 'ensure' in paragraph 1 on page 13 means to:
   A. achieve
   B. make active
   C. improve
   D. make certain

6. What's unusual about giant panda breeding?
   A. They can conceive very easily.
   B. They can only become pregnant during three days annually.
   C. Scientists understand the details of their breeding.
   D. They can't become pregnant without scientific help.

7. In paragraph 2 on page 16, 'their' refers to the:
   A. keepers
   B. twins
   C. mothers
   D. cubs

8. What is causing the loss of the pandas' habitat?
   A. People are cutting down forests to make towns.
   B. Pandas are eating too much bamboo.
   C. The plants in the wilderness are dying.
   D. The pandas are not reproducing at all.

9. A suitable heading for page 23 is:
   A. Songs Save Children from Giant Panda
   B. Education Is the Only Solution for Pandas
   C. Endangered Animals Hurt by Children
   D. Program Teaches Youth Important Lessons

10. The word 'established' on page 24 can be replaced by:
    A. created
    B. brought
    C. admired
    D. guarded

11. Xiaoping Wang's team is planting new trees _____ the earth.
    A. over
    B. in
    C. at
    D. on

12. Wang's project will help pandas by:
    A. increasing the number of animals in China
    B. designing a new kind of bamboo for them to eat
    C. creating an environment that they can live in
    D. teaching people that the panda is a national treasure

HEINLE Times

THE ENDANGERED AFRICAN RHINOCEROS

By Thomas Grant

Africa is home to two of the world's five species of rhinoceros, or 'rhinos': the black rhino and the white rhino. Sadly, both are endangered. Although there are currently slightly more black rhinos, the total number of black rhinos has gone down by more than 90 percent over the past 60 years. Despite a slight increase in the number of black rhinos since 1995, they are still considered to be in danger of completely disappearing. Unfortunately the situation is even worse for the white rhino.

horn

A Black Rhinoceros

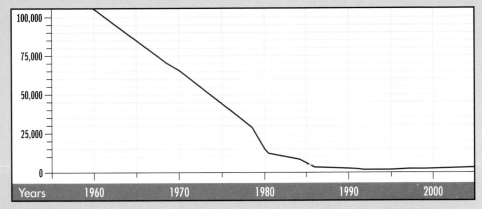

Black Rhino Population from 1960 to 2005

Despite their names, both species of rhino are actually gray. A rhinoceros can weigh between 900 and 1,800 kilograms and can be up to 3.7 meters long. One of their most distinctive features is the large horn, or horns, on their heads. Black rhinos have two horns, one of which is often over 1.2 meters long. These horns are useful for the rhino when it has to defend itself in a fight. However, these same horns are also the reason why so many rhinos are killed each year—not by other animals, but by humans. Rhino horn has been used as a medicine for over 4,000 years, especially in Asia and the Middle East, and demand continues to be very high today. Trading in rhino horn has been illegal for over 20 years but many people ignore this law.

Groups like the World Wildlife Federation (WWF) are trying to protect the remaining rhinos. They're also trying to increase the number of black and white rhinos born each year. This group supports a program to end the buying and selling of rhino horn. It also promotes using alternatives to medicines made from horn. The WWF is working to protect and widen the habitats where these rhinos live so they can survive and safely raise their young. In some cases, they have been able to move groups of animals from a dangerous environment to a safer wilderness area. Without the help of concerned individuals and groups around the world, these species could disappear entirely. If you would like to do something to help save the rhino or other endangered species, contact your local conservation society today.

CD 3, Track 08

Word Count: 360
Time: _____

Vocabulary List

bamboo (2, 3, 19)
breed (2, 4, 10, 13, 14, 16, 27)
conceive (14)
conservation (2, 20, 23)
cub (2, 3, 4, 6, 9, 13, 16, 17)
deforestation (3, 19)
endangered (2, 3, 10, 19, 23)
geneticist (2, 10)
give birth (2, 16)
habitat (3, 10, 19, 23)
obligation (10)
pregnant (2, 14)
rear (16)
reforest (24, 26, 27)
reproductive (13, 19)
treasure (10, 11)
twin (16)
vet (16, 17)
wilderness (3, 19, 20)